# SILHOUETT
# CUTTING

## Marianne Perlot

FORTE UITGEVERS

# Contents

Fourth printing July 2003
ISBN 90 5877 130 x

This is a publication from
Forte Uitgevers BV
P.O. Box 1394
3500 BJ Utrecht
The Netherlands

For more information about the
creative books available from
Forte Uitgevers:
www.hobby-party.com

Editor: Marianne Perlot
Final editing: Hanny Vlaar
Photography and digital image editing:
Fotografie Gerhard Witteveen,
Apeldoorn, the Netherlands
Cover and inner design:
Studio Herman Bade BV, Baarn,
the Netherlands
Translation: TextCase, Michael Ford

# Foreword

A few years ago, I was asked what would be a reason for me to write a hobby book. I then said, "If I have something nice that I want to show others". I thought about this when I was writing this book. This is one of the nicest things I have done in the last few years. My favourite card was also my first: the triptych card with two cut-out patterns and a pretty 3D scene in the middle. Since you can also leave the card standing open (light can then shine through the cut-out silhouette), it is also nice to decorate the inside of the card.

I would like to show you what you can do with these new stencils.

But be careful, it's very addictive.

# Techniques

### What is silhouette cutting?

Silhouette cutting is a simple technique where you cut out the outline of figures or text from paper using a silhouette stencil. You can follow the outline of the stencil with the knife or draw round the stencil with a propelling pencil and then cut along the lines.

Always cut out the lines on the inside before cutting round the outside of an image. If you do it the other way round, you have less grip and the paper will tear more easily. Use a ruler to cut along straight lines and regularly change the blade of the knife.

### Photo 1:

Using non-permanent Scotch Magic Tape Blue, stick the stencil on the card where you wish to cut out the image. Make sure you use a sharp pencil. Use a hard pencil (HB) or a propelling pencil.

### Photo 2:

First, cut out all the shapes inside the silhouette and then cut out the outline and the straight lines. Use a ruler to cut out the straight lines. Practice cutting with the knife to find a way that you find comfortable. Keep turning the paper so that it is easy to cut.

### Photo 3:

Decorate the front of the card using appropriate 3D pictures. Also use a bit of glitter glue here and there.

### Photo 4:

Do not forget to also decorate the inside of the card. You can see through the cut-out area when the card is closed, but you can also display the card standing open.

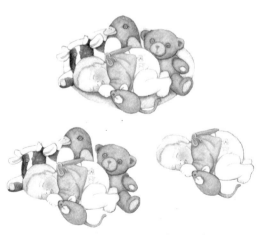

Baby cutting pattern

1. Stick down the stencil and draw round it.

2. Cut out the figures.

3. Decorate the front of the card.

4. Also decorate the inside of the card.

## Making pop-ups

You can use the figure stencils to make pop-ups (see Dolphins, page 29), but text is more suitable for this. Take a sheet of paper and score along the middle fold. Place the stencil exactly in the middle. You can put a dot in the middle of the stencil using a permanent felt-tip pen. Place this dot on the sides. Stick down the stencil using Scotch Magic Tape Blue and draw round it. Cut out the text. If you are dexterous, you can cut out the text directly, but drawing round the stencil and then cutting it out is just as effective. I cut out the corners first and then the straight lines.

Next, place the ruler along the top and bottom edges of the text and cut away the space between the letters. Once all the space between the letters has been cut away, place the ruler along the top and bottom edges of the letters again and carefully score the top and bottom of the letters. Cut a strip which is 1.8 cm wide and 20 cm long from thick card. Slide this strip under the letters which you have cut out and push the bottom forwards. Carefully fold the card closed and then open it again. The texts will now pop up and you can stick this card in another card and decorate it further.

Tip: If you want to punch out shapes, do this before cutting out the silhouette. I once did it the other way round and if the corner punch does not work out as intended, all the cutting you have already done will be wasted.

Another tip: If, in your enthusiasm, you accidentally cut out all the letters with one stroke of the knife, cut them all out and stick them on the card. I did this once, and the baby card on page 17 is the result.

## 3D cut-outs

The 3D cut-outs are made from two or three layers. The cut-out patterns are very easy and most are shown in this book. Use a piece of 3D tape to stick down the layers. Also use 3D tape if you only stick a single layer on the card. You can also use 3D glue if you prefer.

# Materials

☐ Silhouet® stencils
Stencils with figures or text combined with figures. You can also leave out the figures from the text stencils or design your own edge using these figures. You can make your own text or names using the alphabet stencil.

☐ Hobby knife
A special knife which is very thin and very sharp. Make sure the blade is secure and the handle sits nicely in your hand.

☐ Propelling pencil
A long, thin propelling pencil. Suitable for drawing round silhouette stencils. You cannot get into the small corners using a normal pencil.

☐ Silhouet® 3D cutting sheets
Cutting sheets with border patterns which can be combined with the text and figures from the silhouette stencils. The borders can be used horizontally, vertically, as well as diagonally, or each picture can be used individually.

☐ Cutting mat
Choose a good quality mat, because it will be used a lot.

☐ Coloured paper
Use at least 160 gram paper if you wish to cut the card. Artoz paper has been used in almost every example given in this book.

☐ 3D tape
Scotch assembly tape works the best. This can be recognized by its green diamond shape.

☐ 3D scissors

☐ Scotch Magic Tape Blue
This tape has the same sticking force as yellow Post-its and it never damages the paper.

☐ Glitter glue

☐ Multi-tinted paper
Can usually be purchased in a pad. It is available in many different attractive colours. It can be used as a background, but is also very good for cutting.

Tips:
Duo-colour paper and Lacé paper are also very good to use when making these cards.
The high triptych cards fit into a standard envelope and can be easily sent in the post.

# Tulips

*Warm yellow is very suitable for making these sunny, spring cards.*

*What you need:*
- ❏ *Silhouette stencil: Tulip*
- ❏ *Cutting sheets: Meadow 3D background (3DA3306) and Young animals (3D390)*
- ❏ *Paper: Sunny yellow (no. 247) (by Artoz)*
- ❏ *Duo-colour paper: Yellow and green*

You can fold the triptych card closed and tie a ribbon round it. Write the name and message on the back of the card or on a label and tie it to the ribbon.

## 1. Tulip triptych card
Score an A4 sheet 9.8 cm from both short sides and see whether you can fold the card. If so, cut off a strip which is approximately 4 cm wide. The card, which is folded into three sections, then measures 10 x 17 cm and can be sent in a standard envelope. Draw the tulips on the card and cut them out. Stick the 3D background to

the middle section and stick geese and other appropriate 3D images to the background. Use a small piece of tape for the butterfly and fold the wings upwards to give a natural effect.

## 2. Tulips in the meadow
Cut an A4 sheet of duo-colour paper through the middle and fold the card double so that it measures 10.5 x 15 cm. Fold the card open and place the stencil against the line of the fold.

1.

2.

3.

Draw the tulip and cut it out. The duo-colour paper gives an extra, nice effect. Cut out a couple of images from the 3D cutting sheet and make an attractive scene on the inside of the card. Stick some appropriate figures on the front of the card. Use 3D tape to stick on the figures; they can be made into 3D images, but this is not necessary. Use some glitter glue on the edges of the clouds (have you noticed that there is a rabbit cloud and a fish cloud?) and the butterflies. The card will then also look nice if it is left standing open.

## 3. Tulips from Holland

Use a square card which measures 15 x 15 cm. Open the card and place the stencil against the line of the fold. Draw the tulip and cut it out. Next, stick a 3D background on the inside of the card against the line of the fold. You can see the background through the opening. There is some space on the right-hand side of the front of the card to stick a suitable 3D figure. You can also stick something inside the card, because this card also looks nice if it is left standing open.

Garden cutting pattern

# Garden

*These cards create*

*a warm summer*

*evening atmosphere.*

*What you need:*
- ❏ *Silhouette stencils: Rose and Goose*
- ❏ *Cutting sheet: Flowers (SIL3D2201)*
- ❏ *Cutting sheets: Garden 3D*
  *background (3DA3305)*
  *and Summer garden (3D388)*
- ❏ *Paper: Honey yellow (no. 243) and*
  *fawn (no. 241) (by Artoz)*
- ❏ *Raffia*

## Rose card

Score lines 9.8 cm from both sides of an
A4 sheet and fold the card closed. Place
the stencil 0.5 cm from the top of the side
flaps and stick it into place. Draw round the
stencil and cut it out. Stick the garden background in the middle section.
Decorate the card with appropriate pictures
from the cutting sheet. Add 3D details as
you wish.

## Goose card

Use a double card which measures 15 x 15 cm.
Cut a goose from white paper and use the edges
of the stencil as a ruler to cut off the paper. Place
the cut-out goose to the right of the centre of the
card. Mark the opening with a pencil and cut
these lines out. Stick the goose exactly behind
the opening. Stick a lighter or darker piece of
paper measuring 12 x 15 cm on the inside of the
card against the line of the fold. Stick a border
on the end. Make sure this border is the same as
or matches the border on the front of the card
and that it can be seen through the opening.
Tie a strip of raffia around the neck of the goose.

# Roses

Let the attractive shape of the cut-out roses and the different tints of the paper speak for themselves.

*What you need:*
- ❏ Silhouette stencil: Rose
- ❏ Cutting sheet: Flowers (SIL3D2001)
- ❏ Paper: White (no. 211), wine-red (no. 519) and pink (no. 481) (by Artoz)
- ❏ Pink multi-tinted paper

## 1. Dark pink card
Cut out a square card which measures 15 x 15 cm (this one was a ready-made by Papicolor). Place the rose stencil exactly in the middle of the card. Draw round the stencil and cut it out. Do not forget to cut out the inside lines before cutting round the edge! Stick the multi-tinted paper on the inside of the card. Cut a piece of card which measures 13 x 13 cm and stick the darker side of the card against the line of the fold. Stick a border of roses on the separation between the multi-tinted paper and the card.

## 2. Large, light pink card
Fold an A4 sheet double. Carefully cut out the rose stencil from wine-red paper and use the outer lines of the stencil as a cutting line. You can now place the stencil exactly in the middle of the inside of the front page and draw round the circumference using a pencil. Now use your transparent ruler and cut an opening around this which is exactly 0.5 cm smaller. For each side, you will, therefore, need to place the ruler so that you can cut the opening 0.5 cm smaller than the square drawn with the pencil. Stick the rose which you have cut out behind the opening. The inside and outside of the card are now nicely finished.

## 3. White card
Fold a cream A4 sheet double. Make the card exactly the same as card 2 above, except that the rose should be cut out of pink multi-tinted paper. You can cut out the roses and petals from

a rose border and use them to make corner patterns. Stick the roses on the card using 3D tape.

## 4. Pink-red card

Cut out a piece of multi-tinted paper which measures 15 x 13 cm. Place the stencil 1 cm from the left-hand edge and draw it on the paper. Cut out the image. Place the cut-out image on the front of the card with the edge of the multi-tinted paper against the middle fold. Mark the inner circumference of the opening on the front of the card and cut it out using a transparent ruler so that it is 0.5 cm larger. Stick the multi-tinted paper on the front of the card. When the card is stood open, a beautiful light pink rose will be seen. Stick a border of roses on the separation between the multi-tinted paper and the card and work it into a 3D image.

## 5. Congratulations

See Techniques for instructions on how to make a pop-up. Cut 10 cm off of a wine-red sheet of A4 card and fold the remaining piece double. This card will now fit into an envelope. Cut out the words "Congratulations" from a piece of white paper which measures 14 x 18.5 cm. Punch out the corners using an ornament punch and stick a rose border under the text. If you have an extra rose, then it looks good if it is stuck on the front of the card.

# Card cover

*What you need:*
- ❏ *Silhouette stencil: Goose*
- ❏ *Cutting sheets: Farmyard 3D background (3DA3307), with appropriate pictures, Garden table (3D392)*
- ❏ *Paper: White (no. 211) and honey yellow (no. 243) (by Artoz)*
- ❏ *Raffia*

Score an A4 sheet 9.8 cm from both sides. Fold the card double. Stick the stencil onto white paper. Draw round the goose and cut it out. Next, use the outside of the stencil to cut off the paper. The paper goose will be exactly the same size as the stencil. Place the stencil 2 cm from the bottom of the outer flaps. Draw the opening with a pencil and cut it out. Do this carefully, because the figure of the goose must fit exactly when you stick the silhouette to the back. Stick the background on the middle section of the card and finish it off using appropriate pictures from the cutting sheets. You can also add a couple of 3D images.

# Birth announcement cards

*If you accidentally cut through all the letters at the same time, stick them on the card individually.*

*What you need:*
- ❏ *Silhouette stencil: Baby*
- ❏ *Cutting sheets: Party decorations (SIL3D2209) and Baby (3D396)*
- ❏ *Paper: White (no. 211) and light-blue (no. 413) (by Artoz), and soft yellow and dark pink*
- ❏ *Pair of pattern scissors*
- ❏ *Pink stamp-pad ink and sponge*

## 1. and 3. Baby pop-up

The basic card measures 10.5 x 15 cm. The yellow pop-up is cut out from a piece of multi-tinted paper (8.5 x 12.5 cm) which has been folded double. The word "Baby" is cut out from the lightest part. The top has been punched out and a safety pin has been stuck onto it. The ducks are stuck on the card in three layers. Cut off 2 cm from the long side of the double folded white pop-up using a pair of pattern scissors. Dip a sponge into an inkpad and carefully brush the ink around the edge. Stick the white pop-up on a white card and stick the nappy-safety pin border on both sides. You can cut out all the pins and stick them onto the card to make a 3D picture, but a single layer looks nice as well. How to make a pop-up is explained in Techniques.

## 2. Baby blue

Stick the stencil on blue paper. Draw round the stencil and cut it out. Use the outer edge of the stencil as a ruler to cut the silhouette to the

correct size. Place the silhouette on the front of the card and mark the corners of the opening. Join these together using a pencil and cut out the rectangle that you have already made so that it is 2 mm larger. You will be able to see a 2 mm wide blue frame when you stick the text behind the opening. Make an opening in the ball near the duck using an eyelet punch and tie a ribbon through it (the bottle border has an extra layer).

## 4. Yellow baby card

The yellow card measures 15 x 15 cm. The white square with the punched out corners measures 11 x 11 cm and the blue square measures 12 x 12 cm. Unfortunately the yellow text was cut out with too much enthusiasm, but you can still make a pretty card if you stick on the loose letters. The baby is stuck on the card according to the cutting pattern.

## 5. Blue baby card

Cut off 10 cm from an A4 sheet and fold the remaining card double. Take a rectangle of cream paper which measures 8.5 x 19.5 cm. Draw the word "Baby" on the top half and cut it out. Draw the duck on blue paper and cut it out. Make an opening in the ball using a punch and tie the duck like a rattle onto the tail of the last letter of the word Baby. The baby with the full belly is stuck on according to the cutting pattern (page 4).

## 6. Pink baby card

Use a pink card which measures 15 x 15 cm and a white square which measures 13 x 13 cm. Place the stencil 0.5 cm from the top of the white card and draw round the figure. Cut it out and punch an opening in the ball above the duck so that you can put a bow through it. Stick it on the pink card and add a 3D figure of a sleeping baby (see the cutting pattern on page 4).

# Lovebirds

*Wedding cards with a touch of humour.*

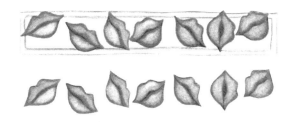

- ❏ *What you need:*
- ❏ *Silhouette stencils: Goose and Love*
- ❏ *Cutting sheet: Party (SIL3D2203)*
- ❏ *Paper: White (no. 211), red (no. 517) and royal blue (no. 427) (by Artoz)*
- ❏ *Glitter glue*

## 1. Love

See Techniques for instructions on how to make a pop-up. Score the middle of a rectangular piece of red paper which measures 13 x 18 cm. This will then fit in a standard-size card (A5 sheet folded double). Do not forget to punch out the shapes before cutting out the text. Stick the kisses border to the bottom of the card and make 3D pictures of the kisses. Put a bit of glitter glue on all the lips.

## 2. Goose with hearts

Use a standard white card and stick the stencil against the right-hand edge. Draw round the stencil and cut out the silhouette. Stick the heart border on the card alongside the silhouette and make the hearts 3D. This can be done using two layers, or even three of four. Stick a royal blue rectangle measuring 9 x 15 cm behind it. Make sure the edge lays against the line of the fold and stick the wedding ring border on the separation between the blue and white. Here, it looks nice if you only work the top or bottom rings into 3D images. You can put some glitter glue on the top wedding ring (like a diamond).

## 3. Lovebirds

Cards like this are always made by accident. Two cut-out geese were accidentally laying next to each other, but you can also do this intentionally. Stick the stencil onto a sheet of white paper and draw round it. Turn the stencil over so that the inside edge lays against the outside edge of the first drawing. Now draw the other goose. Cut both geese out. Give the bride a bow and the groom a tie. This double card measures 16 x 21 cm. An opening measuring 11.5 x 12.8 cm has been cut out of it, but you will have to check whether the geese which you have cut out fit behind it.

1.

2.

3.

The opening in the red card is slightly smaller than the opening of the cut-out geese. In this case, I did not want to see a white border; the geese now literally stand in the opening in the card. Punch out a border along the opening and cut a 1.5 cm wide border around the geese. Stick the geese to the back of the card. Multi-tinted paper does not look as nice with the white geese, because there is not enough contrast.

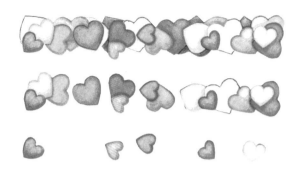

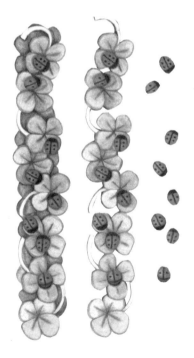

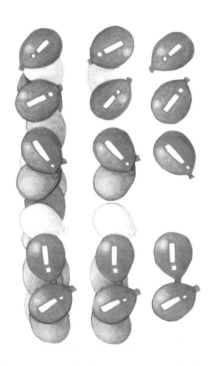

# Geese

What you need:
- Silhouette stencils: Geese and Party
- Cutting sheets: Party decorations
  (SIL3D2203) and Flowers
  (SIL3D2201)
- Paper: White (no. 211), red (no. 517),
  royal blue (no. 427) and birch green
  (no. 305) (by Artoz)
- Glitter glue

## 1. Lucky goose

Use a standard white card and stick the stencil against the right-hand edge. Draw round the goose and cut out the silhouette. Stick bright-green paper (9 x 15 cm) to the inside of the card. Stick the edge of the green paper against the middle fold and stick a border of clover with ladybirds on the separation between the green and white paper. The ladybird border on the front of the card has been made using three layers. You could also add 3D varnish to the ladybirds for an extra effect.

## 2. Party pop-up

See Techniques for instructions on how to make a pop-up. Fold a blue card double and cut off 1 cm from the short edge and the long edge. Place the ruler at an angle with one side 9 cm from the middle fold and the other side 5 cm from the middle fold and cut along the ruler. Stick the balloon border on the bottom and make it into a 3D image. Let a couple of loose balloons fly upwards, but stick them on with 3D tape.

## 3. Party animal

Don't be a silly goose by drink-driving. Drive safely! An azure inside combines nicely with the balloons. This card is made in the same way as card number 1. The only difference is that the stencil on the front of the card is now placed on the left-hand side.

## 4. Silly goose

This silly goose cannot choose between the flowers and the berries. But two things are sure: the card is made in the same way as card number 3 and the lilac paper goes really well with the berries and the balloons. Stick the tulip border to the card using glue and stick a second layer of tulips on top of it.

# On the water

It is wonderful to be on
the water in a boat.
What more do you need?

*What you need:*
- ❏ *Silhouette stencil: Boat*
- ❏ *Cutting sheet: General (SIL3D2202)*
- ❏ *Paper: Red (no. 517), dark blue (no. 417)
  and royal blue (no. 427) (by Artoz)*
- ❏ *Multi-tinted paper (blue)*
- ❏ *Glitter glue*

## 1. Dolphins
Fold an A4 sheet double and stick the stencil in
the middle of the card. Draw round the stencil
and cut out the boat. Stick the dolphin border
under the waves and work the dolphins into 3D
images. Cut out a couple of extra dolphins and
make them jump out of the water. Use the glitter
glue to give the white crests of the waves extra
shine. Also draw drops of water under the dolphins that jump out of the water. Stick blue multi-
tinted paper to the inside of the card and draw
waves on the bottom using glitter glue.

Also stick a dolphin jumping out of the water
here.

## 2. Red and blue card
Fold a red A4 sheet double. Cut a rectangle which
measures 11 x 18 cm from royal blue paper. Cut
out the silhouette of the boat from scraps of dark
blue paper, cutting along the outside edge of the
stencil. The cloud and the waves have not been
drawn in this case and will, therefore, not be cut
out. Next, take a sheet of polystyrene foam (you
may use a washed dish which has been used to
display meat products) and cut out a rectangle
which measures 7.5 x 14.5 cm from it. Place the
silhouette on it and mark the edges of the
opening. Cut out the opening slightly larger. If
you stick a transparent sheet on top of the polystyrene foam and stick the silhouette on top of
it, you can make a shakeable card.

I did not do this with this card. The polystyrene foam has only been used to give the card some depth, because the boat which has been cut out is stuck on the front of the card. Use a piece of multi-tinted paper as a background. Make sure that the change in colour of the paper can be easily seen to create an horizon. The sun and the clouds are made from a border.

### 3. Small red card

Cut 10 cm from a red A4 sheet and fold the remainder double. Cut the silhouette of the boat out of dark blue paper and use the outer edge of the stencil to cut off the paper. Place the silhouette in the middle of the card and mark the edge of the opening. Cut this out so that it is 2 mm larger and stick the boat behind it. Stick a piece of multi-tinted paper which measures 9 x 20 cm on the inside of the card.

Decorate this with a boat, cloud or fish. Part of a border has been stuck on the front of the card. The boats have been cut out again and stuck onto the card using 3D tape. Do not forget to make the crests of the waves shine in the sun.

### 4. Square card

Fold a square card which measures 15 x 15 cm. Place the stencil 1 cm from the right-hand edge and only draw round the boat. Cut it out carefully. Stick on the boat border and make the boats into 3D images. Stick multi-tinted paper which measures 13 x 14.5 cm to the inside of the card. Stick the paper a couple of mm from the top edge and stick a wave with boats on the separation between the light and dark paper. This border does not have to be 3D, but the waves could be made to sparkle.

# Dolphins

You can make them swim

or even jump.

*What you need:*
- ❏ *Silhouette stencil: Dolphin*
- ❏ *Cutting sheet: Beach 3D background (3DA3308) and Marine animals (3D394)*
- ❏ *Paper: White (no. 211), sky blue (no. 391), aquamarine (no. 363), algae green (no. 367) and pastel blue (no. 413) (by Artoz)*
- ❏ *Multi-tinted paper*
- ❏ *Eyelet punch for the eye of the dolphin*

## 1. Aquamarine card

This card should be positioned so that the dolphin jumps out of the water. The card measures 15 x 15 cm and the dolphin is made as a pop-up. Take a piece of paper measuring 17 x 15 cm and stick the stencil 4 cm from the edge using Scotch Magic Tape Blue. Draw round the dolphin and cut it out. Score along the top and bottom of the stencil and score another line 1 cm above the top line. Fold the line under the dolphin towards you. Fold the first score above the dolphin away from you and the line above that towards you. Cut off the edges using a pair of pattern scissors. Fold a piece of scrap algae green paper double and stick the dolphin on it 1 cm from the line of the fold.

Fold the dolphin as it has already been pre-folded and fold the card double. You can now see where the top has to be stuck. You can cut off this dark border and stick it into a double card.

The colours combine very well with fish borders. You can make this into a 3D image (only cut out the fish again).

## 2. Triptych card

Score a line 9.8 cm from the sides and see whether you can fold the card double. Place the stencil 1 cm from the top of both inner flaps and cut out the dolphins. Stick the beach background to the middle part of the card and decorate it with images from the appropriate cutting sheets to make it look nice. All the images have been made 3D. You can make the crests of the wave sparkle using a bit of glitter glue.

### 3. Seals

This is one of my favourite cards. Take a square piece of light blue card which measures 15 x 15 cm and place the stencil 0.5 cm from the right-hand side. Draw round the dolphin and cut it out. Stick the beach to the inside of the card (on the right-hand side so that you can see it through the opening) and stick appropriate 3D figures on the part of the card that the dolphin has not been cut out from. You can also decorate the inside of the card using appropriate figures, because the card also looks nice if you leave it standing open.

### 4. Algae green card

A standard card (an A5 sheet double folded) can also be used to cut silhouettes. Place the stencil against the right-hand edge of the card. Draw

the dolphin and cut it out. Next, stick a piece of sandy yellow multi-tinted paper measuring 14.7 x 9.5 cm against the middle fold. Trim it so that the light side lays against the middle fold and the dark side lays on the right-hand side. Stick the shell border on the separation line.

### 5. White dolphin

This is also a standard card. Place the stencil 0.5 cm from the line of the fold. Draw round the dolphin and cut it out. Cut off 1.5 cm from the bottom of the card and stick the blue multi-tinted paper against it. Make sure the light side lays against the line of the fold. Stick the wave with dolphins under the white dolphin. It now looks as if the dolphin is jumping over them. Work the dolphins into 3D figures and make the crests of the waves sparkle.

# Butterflies (page 1)

*Cover part of the stencil using adhesive tape and use only one butterfly.*

*What you need:*
- ❏ *Silhouette stencil: Butterflies*
- ❏ *Cutting sheet: Flowers (SIL3D2201)*
- ❏ *Paper: Sunny yellow (no. 247) (by Artoz) and purple (no. 46) (by Papicolor)*
- ❏ *Multi-tinted paper*
- ❏ *Glitter glue*

## Yellow card

Cover part of the stencil using normal adhesive tape. Draw round the remaining butterfly in the middle of the card (15 x 15 cm, although it can be smaller) and cut it out. Cut off a piece of multi-tinted paper measuring 14.5 x 13 cm with the light colour on the bottom. Stick this to the inside of the card a couple of mm from the outside edge of the card. Stick a border of butterflies on the separation between the blue and yellow. This card looks really pretty if it is left open. Work the butterflies into 3D images. Stick small strips of 3D tape under the bodies of the butterflies so that the wings can be folded upwards. Use glitter glue on the wings.

## Purple card

Stick the stencil exactly in the middle of the card. Draw round the butterflies and cut them out. Cut off a piece of multi-tinted paper measuring 13 x 14.5 cm with the dark colour on the bottom and stick this a couple of mm from the outside edge of the card. Stick the flower border (purple and pink tulips) on the separation between the multi-tinted paper and the card. Cut out the butterflies from the border and stick them onto the card with a strip of 3D tape under the body. Decorate the wings with a bit of glitter glue.

# Christmas

Make the snow and ice-crystals glisten with glitter glue.

*What you need:*
- ❏ *Silhouette stencil: Christmas tree*
- ❏ *Cutting sheets: Christmas (SIL3D2204) and Winter landscape background (3DA3303)*
- ❏ *Paper: White and fir green (by Artoz)*
- ❏ *Multi-tinted paper*
- ❏ *Glitter glue*

## 1. Snowmen
Use a card which measures 15 x 15 cm. Place the right-hand edge of the stencil 2.5 cm from the right-hand edge of the card and stick the stencil to the card. Draw round the Christmas tree and cut it out. Cut off 2 cm from the right-hand edge. Stick a piece of dark blue paper which measures 14.5 x 14.5 cm on the inside of the card. Tear a hill from white paper and stick a winter scene on it.

## 2. In the forest
Use a green card which measures 15 x 15 cm. Stick the stencil exactly in the middle of the card and draw round it. Cut out the stars first and then the circumference of the tree. Stick a Christmas tree border on both sides and make a 3D image using three layers. Stick light blue multi-tinted paper which measures 15 x 15 cm on the inside of the card.

## 3. Ice-crystals
Cut the Christmas tree out off a standard card. Place the stencil 0.5 cm from the line of the fold and decorate the right-hand side with ice-crystals. Stick blue multi-tinted paper inside the card.

## 4. White Christmas
Take an A4 sheet and score lines 9.8 cm from the edges. Stick the Christmas tree stencil 1.5 cm from the bottom of the card. Draw round the tree and cut it out. Repeat this on the other side. Stick the background to the middle section and cut out the foreground, the reeds on the riverbank and the windmills again.

## 5. Green Christmas
Cut 10 cm off of an A4 sheet and fold the remaining piece double. Place the stencil 1.5 cm from the top of the card. Only draw round the circumference of the tree and cut it out. Only cut out the candles and stick them in the tree. Cut the border with poinsettias to size and work

the white flowers into 3D images. Stick soft-yellow multi-tinted paper inside the card and decorate it with loose poinsettias.

The materials can be ordered by shopkeepers from:
Kars & Co. B.V. in Ochten, the Netherlands.